# Sowing the Wind

Poetry by Edward Foster

*The Space Between Her Bed and Clock*
*The Understanding*
*All Acts Are Simply Acts*
*Adrian as Song*
*boy in the key of e*
*Saturnalia*
*The Angelus Bell*
*Mahrem: Things Men Should Do for Men*
*Selected Works* (Russian translation)
*What He Ought to Know: New and Selected Poems*
*Kar naj bi on vedel* (Slovenian translation)
*A History of the Common Scale*
*Febra Alba* (Romanian translation)
*The Beginning of Sorrows*
*Dire Straits*
*Sowing the Wind*

# Edward Foster

# Sowing the Wind:
## A Requiem in the Modern World

"For they have sown the wind, and they shall reap the whirlwind."

—Hosea 8:7

Marsh Hawk Press · East Rockaway, NY · 2016

12 13 14 15 7 6 5 4 3 2 1 FIRST EDITION

Marsh Hawk Press books are published by Poetry Mailing List, Inc.,
a not-for profit corporation under section 501(c)3 United States
Internal Revenue Code.

Printed in the United States of America.

Library of Congress Cataloging-in-Publication Data

Foster, Edward Halsey, author.
  Sowing the wind : a requiem in the modern world / Edward Foster.
First edition. | East Rockaway, NY : Marsh Hawk Press, 2016.
LCCN 2016028621 | ISBN 9780996427548 (paperback)
BISAC: POETRY / General.
LCC PS3556.O7592 S69 2016 | DDC 811/.54--dc23 LC record

Publication of this book was supported in part by a generous grant from the
Community of Literary Magazines and Presses via the New York State Council on
the Arts.

For Roy and Chris

Ah, when to the heart of man
Was it ever less than a treason
To go with the drift of things,
To yield with a grace to reason,
And bow and accept the end
Of a love or a season?
—Robert Frost, "Reluctance"

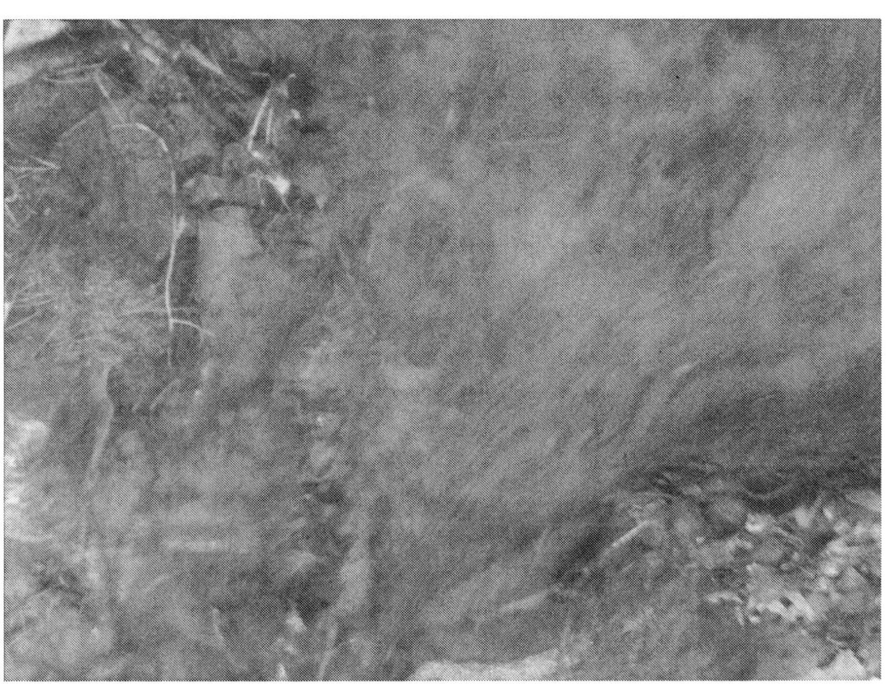

# I. Release

Ecstasy: "4. An exalted state of feeling which engrosses the mind to the exclusion of thought . . . ." —*The Oxford English Dictionary*

*Having wanted so much,*

Aquinas reasoned that
certainty was a mirror.

This image, purely image, gave concern,
awareness, knowledge, things we're living for.

Be as I'd be, cool,
arraigned, hospitable,
withdrawn, captured, sad.

Welcome! Join the motion:
abstractions sweeping back and forth.

Confirm your silence.
The image itself must speak.

Reach in, touch glass,
embrace your speculation,
make it fine.

Place the mirror here
beside yourself.
That is your wine.

This spectacle.

Proceed.

----------

Age is linked to loss,
a way to forget
all knowing,
what has gone.

No longer knowing
who made
this or that.

Your hands will be dust.
You repeat
what you say.
That is no gain.

Loss begets loss.
You are what was,
wondering loss.

The poem is a history.
It is not knowing.
It is not conscious of change

yet is nothing but change.
What is stable is unfelt
but needed again.

You watch blood flow
from the wounds
on your wrist.

What's left
will be paved
and paved again.

The traffic is gone.
It is pointless to call.

There is reason,
anxious of failure.

The fire in your wrists
consumes what you are.

Another time:
all was bustle,
world without end.

Let me rest,
review where the moment
began,

forgetting the prison,
the chance to run wild.

This new world:
no god but thought.
Abstractions haunt Olympus.

Language may say
what to feel,
not what is felt.

Do not believe
what is said,
but say it: thought
is the promise of form.

What's imagined
alters the road,
the map,
the recalcitrant hand,
the one you embrace.

Never travel again.

Your hands are calloused.
The fire is gone.
Your hands are cold.
Light mystifies dark.

Hear breath in the heat.
Recall things that you were.
Form is not felt.
Marble is stone,
manifests form.

----------

1.

Feeling without anything felt,
drawn into the desert,
to the heart.

Friends scurry away.
No one will care.
No one should care.

(Tell me, Charles,
if it ever was,
        or should I say is,
                it ever ok
to do what
others have done?

I don't think so myself, but
I'd like to know
what your feelings
on this subject
are,
Charles.)

                        ----------

2.

You wonder and,

         oh, come on,

you do nothing of the sort.
For you, all poetry is form,
excusing friendship
where there are no friends
whatever the need.

So listen in case
there's an echo
of what's becoming new.

The birds this morning:
the wren,
the hawk.

No, not even their sound,
or this:
the order of words.

He makes them sound like you.
You make them sound like him.

Sit here above the raucous street,

imagine him.

----------

Here then the vector,
the prospect of joy.


Passive, becoming
a gift for your self,
ecstasy without you
as its cause. Asking too
much, hospitable, kind,
the flavor is sour,
your glance can't be known.


The canal to the river.
Remember the silt.
Watch from the bank.


First,


watching the eyes
shifting
this way and that,
telling us nothing.
Nothing revealed
but sorrow,
reticence,
unable to appease
that sorrow,
knowing how soon,
how very soon,
you must leave.

In that passage,
a vector of joy,
much like a tunnel,
a distance, a cloud,
moving here,
and moving away.
Whom do you trust?

What the chemist
does not know
is what we
want to know.

Nothing of rocks,
nothing of force,
nothing that's steady,
yet a matter of math
— merely a thought
until we become
what we have been made to be.

As if answers were hard
in what we promote.

Let us choose
the source of our years,
the seasons of dance,
the delicate swan,
fictions replete with
the snow,
frozen lakes,

and the evening
comes fast.
Now do you hear
the perfection of turns,
leaps in the air,
and you are my fellow,
dawn has begun.

----------

This is what he wrote in his journal:

*It rained today but not enough to wash away the snow. You think it's quite enough to meet for lunch from time to time, ________ (Fill in a name, the name of any will do. Dear reader, why not use yours?), but then there's nothing that we have to say, and yet we trudge on, word after word. Of course, I'm glad that your friend's back from wherever he went and is calm. That's well and good, and it's the Buddhist way, but you don't care. Look, occasional contact's not enough. Oh, sure, the boats are beating back against whatever wave you want to think, but if you'd nudge physics a bit, we might reach common ground. Why did you do it, after all?*

*The snow! The snow! The plow arrived before I was up, and that was in the dark. The thing I want to tell you is that I found a long strand of hair on my keyboard, and as you know, my hair is very short. How did it get there? Was it yours? This place is haunted, and if it weren't for the radio droning on and on, I'd stop and simply go mad. I'm too much alone.*

*Sitting here and wishing that satisfaction weren't so easily the reward. It's an evil as much as pride, to which, allied, it is a taint. We must not care for selves we merge within our own. The damage that the snow can do or will is fascinating to the boy who climbs the hill to see his further range. Locked within a blizzard of dawn, he falls into the cold and his drawn-out death, finding satisfaction in that further range.*

*We watch the snow and wonder why these other folk, two by two, imagine this. Such that when the avalanche begins, they have to run, or think they do. Look, this thing will never work. And there is nothing to forgive. Look, we have the past, but then, without respect, what's it worth? We're just another substitute or stand-in for whatever's sold today. Success.*

----------

*11*

He'd become pure language but,
like words alone,
could never feel.
Irony remained,
and irony
is felt, not feeling.

He'd hone his questions,
showing us that grammar
yields the answer.

Words, he said,
wrongly,
are objects,
like the residue
that glaciers
leave behind.

But he seemed so sharp
until the weather changed,
and then became as ice.

This happened in another age,
while I looked the other way.
I was wrong.
I was cruel.

Here again is the thing I heard.
What I heard was resonance,
so weak that a dance would leave
us glad for weakness

and the loss of who we are.
This sounds extreme,

but knowing him,
you'd know
the meaning
of that sign.

For once,
or so I like to think,
Heidegger in his
droning way
invited
strong young men,
not Nazis,
and probably gay,
to join him
in that mountain hut
he built from his
aesthetic thought.

What did they do?

Well, he might as well have been
in some forgotten place,
Bellows Falls, we'll say, or Cincinnati,
where the cows are green,
and everyone is married a second time.
It's a place to which I'll not return.

----------

Having been trained this way,
I'm left with photographs of you
that give another chance
to edge along perspectives
in your mind.
You have so many angles!
each promising
another chance to fail, to fall,
to find out things about yourself
you hope
that no one sees.

Oh, nameless one,
come home from
the city of sin,
Cleveland,
whatever.

Meanwhile,
stay away from objects,
learn to breathe again.

----------

And here we have the failure of trust, revisions in my expectations (yours as well?), a sense that is distraught, nothing left to be since nothing was lost aside from what we thought was there. And all was vacant, another wry disclosure: look, words have no thought, although they might if spoken by a poet, and such you were. If only I could say as much to you, what solution would be left to realize, possess, and lose? Refined and distant, like a Celtic cross, which promised more, and more. Promises of what would be, and that is so much more. This was the time of ignorance, when God Himself could be the part revealed — revealing nothing but injunction: be calm, and wait: do not pretend.

And here, transcendent, is the cause, the one excuse, like hands skipping along your flesh, liquid and slow. Yet you assume that this friction, skin enhancing skin, is all you'll ever need. So I bend down, head against sand to honor you, procuring from the light and waves the calm you never give. The time of innocence is gone, a sky lit up by sparks, particles of sun. When I lean down, the memory is strong, the sand is gone, and, in its place, I reconceive the moment I first knew you. Or thought I did.

The fact of being makes your wry, unhappy presence fail. What happens if you don't regard, if you are not the object of another man's regard? The clouds dissolve, and your name's inscribed upon a stone that no one reads. It's a scrawl. The sun will shine, the letters coming clear but never read. Here in the language that I write you'll find the scrawl that hides itself in moss, the moss that hides the name we cannot read.

Technique is that which matters, an incident, is you or I. The lapping waves, the house held up with sticks. What is that dark spot that I do not wish to know, that rests in preparation to be known? I'd rather that the world be organized in words, something to be learned, shifting itself in rhythms, in and out, with things I think I know. And then comes death, releasing all those words once more to make it seem as if they never were.

I see the snow envelop space, becoming form as much as clouds or rivulets running down the hill in spring. The snow is felt as cold. The rivulet as dawn becoming warm, and this is felt but not because I thrust my hand inside this transformation but because I know its nature. This part is felt. And all that is is found without. It hides itself beyond translucent walls, crinkled, raw, deliberate. I'm told again what's there, but what I'm told is wrong. Formless and raw, spring makes the rivulet run.

My ease may come accepting this or that and feeling satisfied. How else could I know the sky except as someone's boundary? Your wry tone falsifies what's there, yet I need it when I desire, though you return to your success, familial and dry. What I need will falsify itself, what's left.

----------

Again, from his journal:

*I have only one wish right now, and that involves my windows, which are not clean. To get them the way I want, I'll have to get my ladder and climb up high above the ground. I'm not afraid of heights, and I would not mind were I were to slip and fall, but I would not want to go to the hospital and spend months recovering. Or not recover at all.*

*Let's be honest. Death is not necessarily bad. The phone won't ring, and the only letters and emails I got today came from people who want this or that. Well, they could go somewhere else if I fell. They don't need me, and if they don't need me, why should I need them? Let's face it, the only connections we need are connections that are mutual. Oh, I know how that sounds. But it's true, isn't it?*

*What's more boring in movies than the boy who chases the girl or the other way around? So then they get married, and they have a divorce. You don't get to see that part, the divorce. But you know it's coming. Either that or the big fight after which they won't speak to each other for a while. And then everything's changed. He's not the he that he used to be, or she's not the she that she used to be. Or probably both unless one or the other is secretive and mean. He or she, the one who loses in a case like this, is just a cinder now, ready to go to work and burn, make a living, have sex. The loser thinks that he or she has acquired depth and is more mature, but actually the soul, or whatever you want to call it, is gone. When you come right down to it, it's just as well the phone won't ring.*

*I have a friend – well, not a friend, just someone I used to know – who teaches in some godforsaken place. He has a wife and children (two or three, I forget how many), but they had a falling out, the wife and he, so he found someone else and was full of joy and told everyone about it. We all smiled, and some of us sent presents, and he wrote some books, which I didn't read. The last time I ran into him, he went on and on about how happy he was. Frankly, like all such men, he'd become a bore, which, to tell the truth, he always was, but we went to dinner, and he paid the bill, so I won't object.*

*I don't think he could ever understand why it would be OK to fall off a ladder, just as long as you never knew anything more after you hit the ground. Think about it. Think about falling. Falling through air. No phones. No husband. No wife. Just air.*

----------

Everything's disordered, not confused (as I feel),
for I don't know why you asked that this be done.
Or did you?
I'll lower my sights and think myself less taut
than how I feel right now, and yet
I know you're watching me,
and then there'll be a knock upon the door
(here's the part I like to dream):
I'll answer.
"Come with me," you'll say.

----------

You learn not to listen to those who cannot hear
but watch as if there were a crucifix imbedded in our lives.
It's theirs, you think, to find our fault.
That gives them peace. That much I told you yesterday.

I've seen this happenstance or that change everything.
Circumstance turns decisions round and round until we do not know
if they're the source of wisdom and its inner light,
or, like a mirror, shows us something that we've seen before.

So you deceive, and I'm the one who thought your truth
went beyond the limits of delight to see that letters, luminous,
could dance a frenzied quiet. All around them, those I know
could share the secrets they've kept so long, the varied
lives they've lived, harkening to ancestral glee. The past.
They knew the things that reason never knows.

This morning by the brook (yes, by the brook and hemlocks,
the very place you mirrored me, I mirrored you)
the murmur wasn't loud at first, but then I felt your arm,
though you weren't there, and heard that murmur, not your voice
and words but just the sound.


----------

Whenever you hear, there is but one path to know, a path that isn't learned but felt, and those who do not know push out, away, knowing the mystery can never be theirs. They strut, perform, would be seen, thus never know the numinous because their work is mere acting as if they did know. Irreducible and calm, the warmth between the sheets is no display. To be in thrall requires that others be sent away. Those who won't re-spond encapsulate the act, ironic. He's writing triads with a lilt. Yes, the sound, and, yes, the passage, but where's the root? Where is the dark?

----------

# II. Counterpoint

"With all New England's earnestness and practical efficiency, there is a long withering of the soul's more ethereal part . . . ."
—Harriet Beecher Stowe, *Sunny Memories of Foreign Lands*

Most people want a sounding board, as have you, as have I. "Agree with everything I say, and you'll be mine," you say. (Though when I want to prove you wrong, you demur, you hesitate.) "Watch how I climb into your bed. Do that, and do it just the way I do. Come: climb right in. Agree with everything I say."

Then follow me in essence, if not words, for within that wall I've found a door that opens to another wall. Anxiety is fashioned like the doors that open to discoveries that hold us still.

When you take this slippery pill (like Alice), it will make you happy once again. Serious and drawn, no dreams but this, you might write songs about folks strolling on the street.

Clothes make the man; the man is what he wears.

And could you tell me who is speaking this time, please?

It doesn't matter. Hear me through.

----------

1.


Then, give me one good reason why this,
or any, friendship, should succeed.
We brought each other flowers,
gifts like wine (if not the best).
And so we cheered ourselves.

Thus I liked the way you cooked.
We said we'd known each other's secrets
years and years, and others thought us
close. And so we were.
But was that all?

And so we sat before the flames.
Your preservation was as deep as silt,
dishonored by admissions
that you had been
where I should go.

Let's meet again.
Within a month?
Or two?


----------

2.

The finish on the table starts to crack.
What to do? How can I resist
when this that cost so much
once more needs help. Because I just
don't care. And that, deep down,
is why we
once were friends,
not now.
Friendship
in your mind
(and mine?)
becomes our
furniture.

----------

[For I remember, Dave, your flesh encased in jeans and your
dark sequined look, moonlight spots across your
frame as we walked through the woods. I recall
your boyish hair and how your boots tramped down
the silvered plants. I would have kissed
had you reached back, but laughing was enough. Had to be.
So you and I were seventeen or maybe more
and now: another classmate dead. This time him,
next time maybe me or you. Where is the flesh that I
would so caress? I feel it, though last year
when we crossed paths, I hardly knew that
grizzled chin was yours. The you from way back then
is with me now. You're gone, but in the
solid air, I hold the early you.]


----------

Tubes keep him going. Dials record his breath, telling us things his poems used to tell. Capsized again while gazing through the fog. (Poems are breath. They are air.) He made embarrassment the norm. Would trust neither nurses nor the wind.

So make your preparations, be like him, without a tube, a pill, and experts knowing how to feel. It's bound to happen, no escape, so let's set down the measures before they pass us by. Close the shutters. Watch the dials. Wait for warnings.

Vague, so very vague, he is scrutinized by nurses yet gives up nothing from his simple ways, the outward signs that he is still alive. His just command is now still there, and feeling is the guide. He'd perpetrate a slow, unmoving death. Remembered fairy tales in which the little boy escaped from clutches that undid his moral cause (meaning that he felt soft anger, thus acting in revenge). Now, let him be a child again, grow old, and, wizened, be like me. Try imagining his fright as when another face comes down and nuzzles him. He feels he had the right to take what he can no longer give. A kiss! See his blinking eyes. This creature, squirming, is the dust we all will be. And just as much as he who smeared contentment on my skin.

His history is desire, known through images and sound. We must not despair; that's stasis, pain composed of failed beliefs. No dreaming. We must suffer: we must know it's real.

He is the keeper of the present age. Oh, yes, I see him in that role. Across the table, asking the usual. And compliments unless you tell him what you've really done. It's all too much, you'd like to say: we once were young and wanted, judged for how we looked. But now, it's what we do, I'd say. He thinks we're who we were. Yet in this friendship, we're the keeper of the present age. But nothing more. We'll know much more someday, and then the age will overcome this cold friendship, too. We might as well take on the role that they assign us now.

Well, he was once so young. Now, anger stains his bed sheets, soil broken by new moral growth. Listen. Hear.

I tried to look and act like him. Did you see that? He thought not, so now he's drawn back quietly into woods where squirrels and snakes are wary of my human step. These creatures have their reasons. Thus often they are singled out and shot. Good heavens! Look how little land they occupy. And yet at times they live! Now think of him, his occupations, and the way he'd dress. Why should we make our way through life with manners no one sees?

I justified my look through his. If I could look and seem that way, why not? Admiration was enough until the land began to slope toward dawn. The sun was half as strong as I'd once thought. His person in the dawn was mist. That was where I wished to go and be, but having lived to see him as I wished, I had no other need, in this bright mist, to find and emulate the person and the walk that he'd become.

Friendship, all he was is closed and lost. See him now as if authority were recognition, not some fruitless reaching out for fame. Who fashioned you, young man, in quiet? The street was his. Gentlemen would vacate any bar or future just for him. In the end, they became the sun that never burns. Their joy arose from knowing they could compromise on care.

Take up his role. Do it now before the craziness begins again. My florid face awaits the bed where no one cares and time goes on, little moments that conceive no joy, or so our friendship from now on must tell. But still we have the shore to stroll along, a place from which to see fish leap, hawks dive down, herons catch their prey.

And no one sees this moment except he, as once he wrote, words flimsy as the sky, though not the sky that we were taught at dawn. Don't grasp the air: it's made by you, no solipsist, but here, beneath the sheets, you laugh and watch the hawk dive down.

The sterile imitations that thus I make, my manners reminiscent, my look composed, might be the way that old men saw us and see us now. I carefully arrange my shoulders, and the walk I now assume was built by generations of the nearly glad. Good fortune should be mine, and I'd be free. Delirious, yet everything that I am now once was he.

Why shouldn't I tell you this? Why exclude, consciously, what I know of him — that you would not reach but happily maintain a grim seniority?

I am the words he sought and said.

In diners, at the movies, and in my bed, he thought to please (as once he said). That's not feeling but protection from a chance assault.

New ways to dress flicker in my mind. Suspicion and delirium come to me in waves. He took his privacy, enforcing mine.

My life is lived in other things than his. I see no dream, knowing him. Friendship is a feint, a fraud. It cannot last. He was a poet, or so he said, lucid, learning what the dharma gave, thus reminding me of genteel ladies on the Hudson, who are gladly left alone.

Thus the flag comes down. We consider dawn. What else is left?

----------

[The centipede has not paid taxes,
does not write mail, nor mow the grass.
He runs from me yet lives where I live
and has secrets when I'm not around.
What does he eat? Is he a he,
and if so, does he want a mate?
How does a centipede make love?
Might he be gay or ambidextrous?
Does he bite, like me, in play?
He's determined, never doubts.
Whatever choice he makes, he does not rest
until the thing is done.
He might have been my friend.
We'd talk, and though he could not speak,
I'd know his words.]


----------

Let's pretend this poet has something to say,
something that won't be greeted with a sigh
and clapping noise.

A chemist of the mind.

Let's pretend that he has more to life than himself
and whomever else he feels will meet his expectations.

Let's pretend that he is more than lost.
Let's pretend that he will care,
reminding you of something you might say.

Let's pretend he's closeted in dark, unfathomed space,
that he's a poet and that he's real.

----------

To sleep is not enough —
Prospero harvests the sea
and, like a seaman, reels us in.
He sees our globes, our eyes.

Fortune tells us all.
The bed is quiet.
The silk is still.

Why shift our cares to him?
His venom has no need.

Our bed is made of damask, our pillows silk.
We sleep while others watch.

----------

First off, I heard him say
he'd never traveled north.
He is the silky thread
that pulls us all up tight,
telling friends exactly
what he thinks they want to hear.
To him I say, beware of words.
They're closer to the earth
than what you think.
They make and verify
your thought.
In their place,
choose wonder.

----------

And from him, guilt: a word to which I turn as often as I analyze the snake and, looking for that part we call his neck, watch him wriggle through the grass, consume a mouse, and, coiling, warn us once again, keep your distance, for I'll lunge and bite. But in my heart I know no fear. And then he enters me.

I like to brush my hand along his mottled head. I like to tweak him by the tail and bring him close. I stare into his eyes, so moist. I'm not afraid, for in his lunge, he'll always miss the mark. Spittle from his lips coats my hand. I treasure him as much as having guilt of this or that. He does not know he is my closest friend.

Farewell to which idea? Mr. Stevens, ideas were never strong: weak plants to cultivate in borrowed soil. But watch the snake, the image of the snake, parting blade from blade, hair from hair. There is such joy as he moves near.

----------

Each room a prison,
containment made from
someone's will or hope.

This is where we rest,
And in this room,
I watch my flowers grow.
I'm rich, and in my hands
his hands will compliment
our rings.

The residue of husbands
I adore. All this you'll find
In books, for they are very rich
in thought.

He says, I'm one with you.
Revolution makes me glad.
My reply begins, Touch my heart.

----------

The poem lets us see what can't be seen, the absence on a hillside, a taste of cold. Daily wonders that have no cause but something gracious, unremembered, hard. These poems ask what cannot be said, hidden and oblique. Poetry is not for scholars, facile in their memories of what they've read, propositions encountered in a gnostic text, symptoms built from knowing, not from what is known. Clever language, clever thoughts. Their words release a harmony of doubt. And is this all they have to say? Alas, with them, this is all there is. We send them back to classrooms. They were meant to teach.

----------

This much is known: my critic, classrooms — sanctified, destructive truth.

For chemistry has figured in my dreams — those formulae, enigmas that exist in thought, redeeming us from guesswork, doubt, and magic words. Technicians hard at work have sought what can't be known.

Lying deep beneath the master, underneath this tree, the sky becomes a blank, nothing but metaphor, ambitions for light, sweet in the air, but his gestures say, No. Down in the reaches of age, I'll imagine a thought, reach under his shirt. Then, what would that be? Only a gesture, only a person of light, falling from the blankness of sky. For this we are told: it's molecules, matters of numbers and charts that correct but redeem nothing at all. Still, we must die, chemists or not. The lab is a crystal of light, dark light. For that is the prize, the failure of physics, the new sanctified truth, taught in the classrooms, taken as light. It's nothing but this, the instructors would say, a form made of things made of things, energy, light. Pity the masters of molecules, form. How little they know. Their matter is made up of math and of books. Their gestures are dark, knowing nothing of sound, but my lover is light, giving me form. How weak is their physics, mechanics, their sanctified truth. Reach down, let them go, reach beneath my shirt.

----------

You try to run but cannot run the way I run,
so fast, my hands embracing, at your back,
meeting tendon, muscle,
though you shake me off, me
and every other man you meet.

You want to be alone and search as if you sought,
and only sought, but then I have you now.
You try to run but cannot run as fast as I.

So what's the use for me?
You only seem to shake away the hands,
the image: hands that seek you out. You say
you only want to seek and not be sought.

And so the meter runs.

But look: turn back and look
and see the one who seeks you out, not because
you dress the way that others do, not because another's
found that I found you. Not jealousy or envy,
but need, my florid friend, my flower, lover,
nightshade, deadly, caught in fright.
Let mine become your words,
enigma, fancy, fraught with need.

If you'd just turn,
one final thrust
of that ecstatic storm
would make us what we are.

----------

The world's complete with ugly folk. As you. As me. Were this not so, coronas around my sun would dim, and waves would wash away my sight of land. Catastrophe is needed to define our motion in the waves. It makes us drown in all that lies ahead. Beneath the surface, I can glimpse the legs of charming men. I swim toward them, faster in pursuit of things I never reach. Land falls away, and I am further in the sea than I have ever been. I never will return. The solitude of waves form and break. The swell of water as I move toward what I see dips down. The image in my mind seems to move much faster now. The land is almost gone. Let me drop into the brine and catch that fleeting sight.

----------

Make embarrassment the norm. Trust neither that
nor weather. But have you made your preparations
without consulting experts knowing how to feel?

It's bound to happen, no escape,
so let's set down the measures
before they pass us by.
Close the shutters.
Watch the dials.
Wait for warnings.
Why should not I talk like this?
Why exclude all I've learned of you —
that you won't reach but happily
maintain a grim seniority?

I am the words you seek and say.


----------

Repeat:


In diners, at the movies, and in my bed,
you think to please (you said).
Not feeling but protection from
a chance assault.

New ways to dress flicker in your mind.
Suspicion and delirium come to mine in waves.
You take your privacy, enforcing mine.

As was said. And said again.

I wish that you'd be coming home tonight,
not just reading poems written years ago.


––––––––––

The day has almost ended, and the flowers gone. Now for weeds, though in this weather (Jesus, but it's cold) what I mostly care about are friends, warm if so confined, within their city homes. What would the Puritans have said about our central heat? No wonder we expect so much.

So many sentiments. So many questions.

----------

Could we be there again? Could we see you as you were?

Look! I've tried to be as you once were. It didn't help.

It took me months to know what you'd present. That's so. Then why so empty? Either you or me. The passengers have left the shore. The boat is gone.

----------

Where can I watch and not be seen?
Where can I count the things for which I care,
not emerge in someone else's sense of who I am?
I used to think I'd meet a man who'd understand.
I thought we'd travel through the night,
along the shore, and know that Rome
would find us in the morning
looking at the monuments
and know our destiny was now.
Romance!
I was so very foolish.
I am so very dumb.


----------

# III. Des Knaben Wunderhorn

"The interior is the asylum where art takes refuge."
—Walter Benjamin, The Arcades Project

Death is certain,
though given time,
cleaning out the attic,
I'll find a clue,
leaving nothing behind
just for you to seek.

Yet if I do it well,
you'll still find secrets
I've packaged there for you.

One thing I've come
to know is last year's
look is out of fashion.

I go on, ignoring what
once brought me here.
I am the one I was.

I clean the attic,
full of dust, old boxes,
the residue of fashions,
bouquets, and
manliness, all there in hopes
that you'd be stopping by again.

But you yourself
are sweet in air,
this box of clothes
you wore.

You're wanting
to close this longing,
young beauty; you now
pirouette in peace.

Not one path or ramble.
(Were you ever there?)
But these are feints,
pariahs (you) (me),
out of our burrow,
into the sun,
our late afternoon sun,
everything there to be seen.

Yet name it, Fox;
tell me
what's to see?

You, my fox,
watching for evening,
wanting to see,
but the air is empty,
the audience gone.

Thus being alone,
knowing there's no one
to care.

And so to dance in the evening,
knowing no one will see.
Ecstasy's feeling, not merely felt.

----------

Don't give in. Not yet. The lava flows about our feet. Basalt walls pretend there's nowhere else to go. We feel what only we can feel. The heat reclaims the ice. Our names are certain, when we say they are. This prison is a hurricane of names. They look like ravens, swept along in vapors above my boiling heat. "I am alone" has lost its fear. In this, trying not to say what I've not seen myself — things like boys in swimming holes, which may exist. — Eakins thought so, but I wasn't there, although I've seen his painting, if only in a book, and hoped I'd swim there someday, and they'd come over, the boys I mean, and make me feel at home.

I think they're like those figures in another work — "Snap the Whip." A schoolhouse in the background, boys holding on, and the painting's set in magic, where you could lie on grass, no longer fearing lyme disease.

Thus constituted — solitary, singing — all sound no more than noise from which to act, not from choice but from what is. So was it that you drove me out of your life, as you thought, only to be heard. Only then could sound be renewed. A flashing, too, a fiction.

And so what came to matter was the make of the wood, the word: the violin, the cello, the bass, sounds that resonate themselves.

Why argue with a learned man, who cannot hear us think?

Aquinas served the church, not God. His answers were like shattered mirrors, full of light, parts of some wholeness we can't reconstruct except as sound. Nothing numbers could resolve.

Sound finds its way around the form and thus is formed itself, echoes of what you or I, whoever, sings.

----------

50

He'd been looking for a friend all day.
There were none.
Fascination turned to things
that could not move or speak.
He watched things grow.
He wandered in the field.
He saw all things looking as they should,
never taut like syntax,
which tilts toward sense.
(Sense, he thought, has
its breeding ground
in shame.)

He had to complicate everything he saw
until he came to think that how he dressed
was how they knew him in the world.

The winter's force and rocks,
the granite cliff:
these things still hold the grasses back.
They held him back.

He cherished figures moving in his dream. Every time they moved away
and called to him across the air, the granite cliff kept him back. He could
not join. He ought to jump,

and in some dream, he may.

Here satisfaction seems as silly
as his plans for spring. The garden
is a mass of grey and brown.

The garden, sleeping now and ever,
is dreamt into reason,
then is gone.

The claimants for marriage
no longer convince, not now,
when all that I can hope is that
they visit again.

Here in the rite of loss,
imagined and self-imagined,
the blinds are drawn,
but the men on the street
are able to see
what none will tell.

Secrets imprison, alone.

Water cascades through the house at night.
Streams reach out toward the hemlocks, the brook.
He is alone with his self
and knows
what the blinds are chosen to hide,
when the summer is dark.

His dream will reach through paper and ink,
slip hands down my neck.
Blinds are made to keep us alone.

Here then is the vector,
the passage to joy.

*52*

Passive, pretentious,
a present we give
to ourselves, and a
language of ecstasy with
none for its cause.

Asking too much,
hospitable, kind,
his flavor is soured,
his glance is unseen.

The brook among hemlocks.
Remember the silt.
Watch from the bank.

But watching his eyes
shifting this way and that,
telling us nothing,
nothing's revealed
but abject sorrow
and reticence,
unable to disguise
that sorrow,
knowing how soon,
how very soon, he must
leave.

Such is that passage,
that vector of joy,
sometimes a tunnel,
a distance, a cloud,

here moving close,
now rushing away.
Whom do you trust?

What the chemist can't know
is what we want to know.
Nothing of force,
nothing of rocks,
or thought
until we are made
as what we've been taught,
as if the answer could be caught
within systems we made.

Such is our need,
our seasons for dance, completion
of snow, frozen lakes, and the evening
comes fast. Now do you hear
the perfection of turns, leaps through
the air, and you are my fellow,
dawn has begun.

----------

1.

That boy sacrificed his ego,
shaved his head,
was humiliated,
and looked into the dark until,
he said, he saw light.

The mind of god, he found, was his.
He was humbled
but knew he had always been right.


----------

2.


The harm that children do,
within imagined worlds
breaks down despair
and makes you reconceive
yourself.


You see him as a child, gracious on a beach,
a fresh and fancy grace that you misjudge.
Error is the rule. And then the waves
wash out his footprints in the sand.


So now, why wait?
Why stick around
to dissipate that past
if you intend no harm.


You have the rope.
You have the beam.


Not true. Not true enough.
The harm was real.


----------

How do you know what you are? My wish for you was not fulfilled. Instead you found the streets to be the perfect place to hurl an insult at those who might have cared. You thought yourself to be another whom we'd wish. You were nothing of the sort. You'd rather let your talents seek out someone else to hurt. Remember Blanche:"Deliberate cruelty is not forgivable."

So why, when you know what I intend to do is cruel, why ask? These secrets that we share are known to few. Stop pretending anything redeems the act we did between these windows and the door. Step close and closer. Leave no room to spare: I don't intend to hurt. I never did.

Here is how it is. I'd been thinking only of the error (mistake, fraud, myself, and you). But if you would confirm the need, step here, beyond the shadows, beyond night. Then on my cheek your hand could push me down. The cushion would give me rest. I'd rest, and the dark flaws that I am, that are you, might be all that we were, vessels drunk in solutions of dark, indeterminate need.

----------

The secret of poems:
to feel with nothing to feel.
No cloud, no storm, no mountain peak,
no Blake, no Whitman, no relief
from all those corporate intersections,
telling whom to hear,
how to feel,
what to know.

Things are never real
until they're caught
and made as thought.
Attention drawn from
bookshelves.

Mirrors are the fictions
that we love:
to look and to see.
His frame moves
in a sideways glance,
as in this wind, light and red.
He forecasts things that
no one hears
and knows,
and yet he speaks,
running his hands along
my savored slick unbroken flesh,
memory reflected from a bar or beach,
and wishes he might not pursue
but be pursued.

What you must say, you have to say.
The glass will glisten, image of the brink
he cannot touch. Morning's now
so far away. The sheets are calm,
and he pursues what's only in his mind.

Now the light is all he needs.
Fiction is the form he could define.
The edge of glass is like the edge of rock
and cannot break.

He cuts his skin, his wrist, again;
his is the perch
on which to lie,
surrounded by a glassy field,
the woods, the darkened sky.

This world redeems his self
when this is what he has to do:
listen to the way the grasses
calm themselves,
so like reflected selves.
That's what it is?
He'd stay at home,
released from spells
and others' expectations,
redeemed by lack of movement,
lack of wind.

He set the meter,
moving language left to right;

the mirror adjusts the increments
until it's he that's found,
wording caught in glass,
a privilege that

must not anticipate the flaw,
the cut upon his wrist.

Not you, who catches
passing light,
but he who
occupies the night.

(We stay outside,
inadequate and cold.)

I try to dress like him
(to be like him),
but then he'll change,
though underneath
remain the same
(a part I cannot reach).

Water washing,
elbow grease,
too late
to think.

And so I come
not to dress for him,
not to be like him.

His weedy humor,
wily, cool, capable
of memory, nothing
as brilliant and sharp
as this morning's wind.

What icicles? I told him,
I came for the opera
of sound.

Then summer in the morning,
crickets seem to answer birds.
Here is the wood thrush,
swallow, robin, finch,
as I lie, keeping
watch, inch by inch,
what he will
never feel
nor hear.

Yet he is my patron
and my love,
while you,
a newer sound,
ensconced
in sullen thought,
await a call,
my call.

No,
any call.

So it is that you and he, poets both, spoke of Dante, how much he knew,
as if his notions were no less today than they had been.

What arrogance does any friendship have, as if our knowing were strictly
in the word? It's in the sound.

(Thus, I read my words over and over, again and again, and see what they
were, making sound,

such that after sex,
useless, bored,
I weed the garden,
cut down the weeds as if
it's what
my hands allow
[hands growing numb].
You see, I gave up seeking.
I'm really not talking with him anymore.)

Let the house change you,
change him.

Stay out of the dream,
cautiously count, counting
as if to be there always,
without count. The clock is all we have,
dreaming made it so.

The water drains the land.
The marsh is deep and soft.
The hemlocks bury us in dark.
The sun won't rise.
The air is heavy.
The mist. The muck
is strong and warm,
forever felt,
but only felt.

How nice it would be to write poems
about things for which people care,
to hear a sign, rustling hands,
to accept this as if due,
accepting it as warmth.
Note what languages did.
They've done it before.

And so I sit here waiting,
this or that, this or that.

What's left to say
when friendship
nears an end?

He, too, will die,
and I'll go on
a while (I hope),
But, look,

the future's not so bright
as once it used to be.
Now it's something
we have learned
to see.

The fire's in the grate.
Night is coming on.
We talk.
We talk.

> Now, this was when we were young, he says,
> and we'd be dressing up in sturdy jeans, like him,
> and then we'd touch and feel the cloth between the skin.
> Pretending to be just like him.

Yes, I know it's easier on the ears
to stick to simple tones
(with variations), but I have to say,
for me, that's not enough.

Who put this fire in my mind,
my mouth,
before I find myself a rope,
a beam to hang it from?

How else to get around the fact
that also he
would die?

----------

*Coda: Details for a Final Dream*

The crowd moves by,
much more to see of what I'd like to see
than merely those who choose to march.
The crowd contains the men he used to be,
decorations for the dreams I'll dream tonight.
I count them friends, images of liquid joy,
not designs put up to teach us care
but soft and fleeting moments in the dark.
Within this dream, they'll be my crowd
of dust.

----------

# IV. The Children of Wrath

"The real is only the base. But it is the base." --Wallace Stevens, "Adagia"

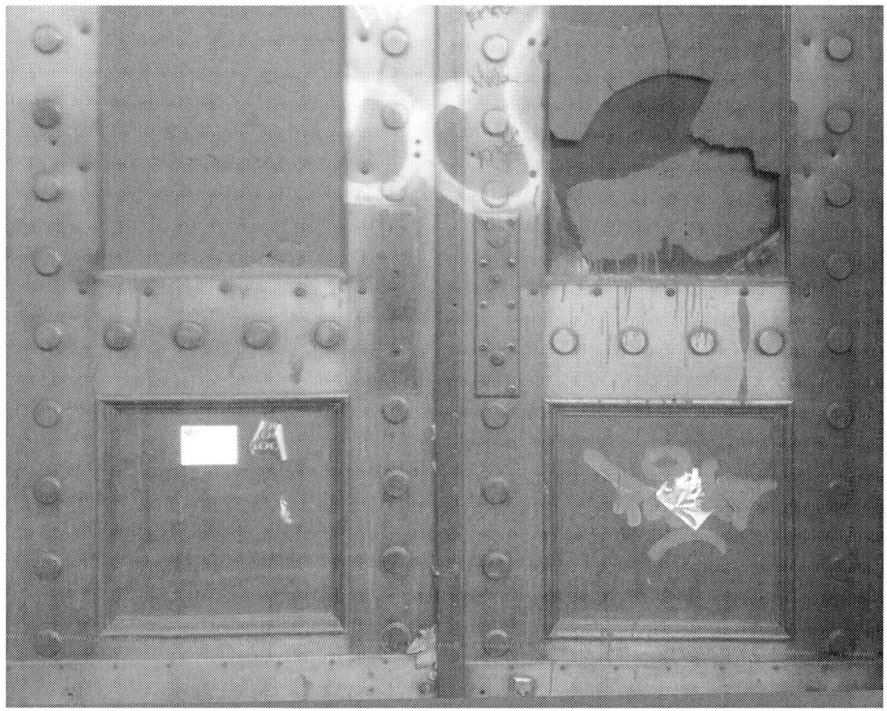

The notion of a direct personal route to truth, an unmediated knowing, without reference to empirical evidence is an absurdity, prized by solipsists who in fact do not know and imagine and assert. Truth is, rather, known through empirical observation and feeling, not through a refreshing inflow of divinity. Emerson's notion of transcendent truth is an invitation to solipsism, fantasy, and self-delusion.

----------

Emily Dickinson's poetry required that moment of gnosis when a set of words — which, as poetry, were as yet nothing in themselves — became the trajectory, the vector that is the poem.

----------

In the chapter entitled "Spring" in *Walden*, Henry David Thoreau finds "the forms which thawing sand and clay assume in flowing down the sides of a deep cut on the railroad through which [he] passed on [his] way to the village." These forms lead him through a series of observations and meditations to recognize, "There is nothing inorganic. [...] The earth is not a mere fragment of dead history, stratum upon stratum like the leaves of a book [...] but living poetry [...]." He reaches his conclusion inductively, not, as had Emerson, because "the currents of the Universal Being circulate through [him]." The strata of the earth are "like the leaves of a book," which Thoreau calls "living poetry."

----------

For Dickinson, correspondence between empirically defined fact and a "higher" truth was crucial. Dickinson was no Emersonian, merging with the great all. Rather, beginning with a firm sense of materiality and fact, her work found correspondence and the trajectory that is the poem itself, in a moment of gnostic awareness, not the gnosis that is supposed to arise from a distrust of the world but the gnosis that follows from a joy in the very things that early gnostics disowned. Thus her poems commonly begin with an observation or statement of fact ("The most triumphant Bird I ever knew or met") and embark on a trajectory that ends with an equivalence, often spiritual or intangible (in this case, "finest Glory"). The poem in effect proposes its own scripture.

----------

Our secular culture is rooted in belief systems and is itself a belief system. What passes as a means to "truth" is grounded in notions that survive from a religious past. These notions have qualified American poetry. They are rooted not in logic but in gnosis.

----------

To move from perception through the poem itself, a key or secret knowing is needed. Sometimes that key is provided by "science" or "pseudo-science" (Freudian theory will do) or linguistics, but this is not true gnosis. Rather, gnosis may involve, for instance, compulsion ("the poetry of dictation") and never, in any case, intention. The poem may entail a perception of something in the world experienced inductively rather than imagined. Gnosis occurs when language becomes more than itself, and correspondence is established. Listen to the words, only the words.

----------

Gnosis, as the word is used here, can be imitated but not learned and is uniquely inflected by the poet's world and being.

----------

Thus, gnosis can be said to have a history but is not itself within history.

----------